TAP DANCING ON QUICKSAND
WHILE
GARGLING PEANUT BUTTER
One family's story of
Walking the AIDS Journey

JON MICHAEL
March 24, 1963 -- July 22, 1994

Sarah Pennington
With Dan Pennington

Sarah Pennington

©2008 by Sarah Pennington

All rights reserved. No part of this book may be reproduced by any means without permission of author except for brief quotations in newsprint, or periodical forms.

ISBN 978-0-6152-1357-6

Printed in the United States of America.

Tap Dancing on Quicksand While Gargling Peanut Butter

Dedication

For my Heavenly Father who loves me enough
to trust me with a little bit of His business.

For Dan, the godliest man I know.

For Stephanie Michelle, Sierra Danielle, and Jonathan Israel,
who know all my failings as a mother and love me anyway.

Acknowledgements

I am grateful to so many people. There are those who walked the journey with me and became characters in my book. If you want to know who your real friends are, choose to walk through adversity. All your fair-weather friends will turn away. You will be left with people like Bruce and Michele Mattson and Paula Van Cott. I was blessed almost every day with the presence of Michele or Paula. On the day my washing machine fell apart, Bruce appeared and installed a replacement. Papa and I treasure their friendships.

I have been blessed to be a part of Stanwood Scribblers, where I receive encouragement, support, and feedback.

My Scribbler buddy, Norm Gubber, fills us all with laughter and generously gave his time to help me navigate the self-publishing highway.

Editor Extraordinaire, Jeanne Bartlett, knows how to move chapters around and make me laugh at my mistakes. Her input in my writing and my life has been priceless.

Then there were those who did a final run-through of the rough draft and made suggestions, comments, and corrections: Karen Anderson, Julie Peddy, Vanessa Lewis, and Dorothy Trueblood.

Papa stepped so far out of his comfort zone to share his feelings with you. He is my Superman, my supporter, my encourager, the love of my life.

Tap Dancing on Quicksand While Gargling Peanut Butter

Preface

When I look back at those long, dreary, too-short days in 1994, I think of what my sorority sister, Barb Cook said. She lost her son, Ken, just before Christmas, 1993 – seven months before I lost mine. She described walking the AIDS Journey as 'Tap dancing on quicksand while gargling peanut butter'. I am convinced she is right. I felt overwhelmed and about to go under. I was always tip-toeing, trying to go faster, struggling for air. I never felt the satisfaction of saying the right thing - seldom knew what to do. I just had to do it.

This is the story of our Journey Home…

Sarah Pennington

March 10, 1980
Maternally in Love

The scrawny, beaten-down young man with the orange-red afro kept his eyes glued to the worn tread of the foyer carpet as the probation officer urged him into the house. Jon Michael was number four in our last mix of teenage foster sons. I fell hopelessly, maternally, in love with him. It would be years before I knew how quickly he had loved me too.

To say he came to us damaged was an understatement. The youngest of nine children, aged two to eighteen, little Jon had been forced to stand in the picture window of his family's rambling farmhouse to stare out into a thunder storm while his father stripped his mother naked in the pasture. The cruel man tied her to a tree which had been struck by lightning several times. As terror swelled in his children's hearts, he yelled, "Watch your mother fry!"

Later, Jon Michael stood in the circle of his siblings around an open grave as his father told his mother, "If you ever cross me, I'll dig this hole three-feet deeper and bury you. They'll put a casket on top of you and no one will ever find you." Turning and pointing his finger at the children in the circle, he added, "And none of you will ever tell."

Jon's afro hair had been an anathema to his dad and justification for accusing mom of infidelity during their many sessions of abuse. Jon Michael's head was consistently shaved until he was fifteen years old. With his lily-white, freckled skin, he had a hard time understanding why his daddy called him "the N word."

When Jon was eleven and his sister was twelve, they went to their Sunday school teacher and told her about the abuse they were suffering at home. Remember, this was the 1970s. This woman brought the two terrified children in front of their church-going, God-fearing daddy and said, "Tell your daddy what you just said about him!"

After a horrific beating, the children were able to escape and hide out in an abandoned farm house for a week. Eventually, with nowhere else to go, they returned home.

During the next four years Jon watched his dad run over his kitten with a threshing machine, kick his puppy into the side of the garage until he was dead, and learned to live his life in constant fear, trusting no one. He and his siblings made several calls to Child Protective Services which went unheeded, because they did not know the necessary verbiage to meet the criteria for intervention.

Tap Dancing on Quicksand While Gargling Peanut Butter

In the fall of 1979, Jon snuck into his sleeping father's bedroom, stole his car keys and $300.00. With trembling hands, he turned the ignition in his dad's brand-new Lincoln and drove to the bus station. Thinking only of getting away from the terror in his life, he purchased an economy ticket to his Grandma Ginger's in California. After living on candy bars for several days, he arrived at his destination and called his grandmother to pick him up.

Jon took a hot, welcome shower. His grandmother prepared a home-cooked meal. Together they sat down in her kitchen nook while he ate and poured his heart out. "Stay here," she offered, but they both knew that Jon's dad would find him and come for him, just like he had in the past. They also knew that, as a teenager, his only ticket out of the abuse was through Juvenile Probation, not CPS.

When Ginger was satisfied her grandchild was clean, refreshed and fed, Jon called the police to turn himself in. He gave the dispatcher his full name and disclosed, "I stole a car and $300 in Ohio. I've broken the law. Please arrest me and put me in a foster home."

To his dismay, Jon was flown back to Ohio and placed in Juvenile Detention. Three months later, he was assigned a probation officer and got his wish. He was placed in long-term foster care in our home on March 10, 1980 – two weeks before his sixteenth birthday.

Sarah Pennington

March 24, 1980
Jon Michael's Sixteenth Birthday

In the 1970s, Farrell's Ice Cream Parlors had swept the nation. The Columbus, Ohio Farrell's was a favorite spot for our foster sons to celebrate birthdays and accomplishments.

We chose to enjoy Jon Michael's sixteenth birthday there. Seated at a booth like the one pictured below, Jon found himself sandwiched in the middle with foster brothers on either side of him. My husband and I sat in the two chairs and 20-month-old Sierra squirmed joyfully in a highchair at the end of the table. Jon had never been to a Farrell's and did not know what to expect.

Without warning, the wait staff noisily approached our table complete with an Energizer bunny-style marching bass drum, singing the Farrell's version of Happy Birthday. To our chagrin, Jon Michael slid underneath the table while the other boys convulsed in laughter. Papa and I were heart broken that our special treat was a traumatic experience for this wonderful young man.

When Jon realized how foolish he looked, crawling under the table at sixteen, he was too embarrassed to come out. I spoke to the staff, who politely prepared our ice creams to go and boxed our cake. Meanwhile, Papa and the boys helped Jon sneak out from under the table and get out of the restaurant.

Tap Dancing on Quicksand While Gargling Peanut Butter

Puppy

Jon Michael was the forty-seventh – and final - foster child to be placed in our home. Every one of the forty-seven has left an impression of memorable moments on our hearts. Those last four boys, Kenny, James Ed, Larry and Jon Michael kept our home full with friends, laughter and shenanigans. They each deserve their own book. Each is (or would be) in his forties today. Kenny is a successful businessman. We've lost touch with James. Larry died in 1993. He would have been thirty-one-years old.

****

During Jon's first year with us a caseworker recommended intensive therapy. Jon agreed to go only if I attended the sessions with him. This Mama-dependence would continue until his death. It was during those sessions that the horrific memories of abuse came out and became burned into my psyche. 'Our' therapist, Tim, was extraordinary. At the end of one very fruitful session Tim recommended we procure a puppy for Jon. What an ingenious idea: he could now bring a puppy into a safe environment. There would be no abusive father to harm either of them and we all know the therapeutic effects of a pet. Grandma Pennington had new puppies. They were adorable little Beagle-bundles of hyperactive joy with long ears and fat bellies. Jon was in hog heaven, wallowing on the floor with the puppy and little Sierra. I can still hear his voice calling, "Come on, puppy!" I also distinctly recall that not once, not twice, but five times in the first 24 hours, I heard Jon yelling, "No, puppy! Bad puppy!" He wiped the pup's nose in the puddles on my carpet and made foams of carpet-shampoo-polka-dots in my living room.

On Puppy's second morning with us, Jon Michael almost missed the school bus. He was busy frolicking in the back yard with Puppy, when the other boys began yelling for him to come on! Without thinking, Jon opened the gate and left it ajar. He did not notice the tiny beagle ball trying to catch up. Hearing the boys calling for Jon, I looked out the kitchen window just in time to see Puppy darting under the back tire of the bus. Our boys didn't notice. By the time they returned from school, I had prepared Puppy in a gift-wrapped shoe box and we all participated in helping Jon find an appropriate place to bury Puppy. We offered him another puppy from the same litter, but he'd have none of it, telling his therapist in a flat voice, "I wasn't meant to have a puppy. I'll just play with the ones at Grandma Pennington's."

It took Jon ten years to resolve his pet phobia.

Sarah Pennington

The Sixty-Two Fifty

Over the past forty years my husband, Dan, has come to be called Papa. In 1980 he was a full-time student at Ohio State University, while working an evening job at a high-class, up-town hotel. I was working a part-time position for our agency and serving as social secretary for our bustling brood.

We had few funds and a nasty need for a second vehicle. I found the car of my dreams – one which would get me from point A to point B. This was enhanced by the fact that I was able to bargain the seller down from $75.00 to $62.50. The ugly-green, outdated, four-door Ford Fairlane was great for the short ten-minute drives to the office, high school, doctor, dentist and counseling appointments.

Based on her price, the boys named her "The Sixty-two Fifty." Their derision of her was horrendous, referring to her as "Mom's Junker Clunker," and whining, "It's so humiliating to ride in this piece of trash." On those rare occasions when we needed to take both vehicles, the boys piled into the van in a frenzy to avoid riding in her.

The first time Jon, our most finicky of fifty-two children, had to be transported in her; he threw a fit, pointing out that he was sure the front floorboard was crackling when he got in. He ripped back the shabby floor mat, exposing rusty metal which he proceeded to kick loose until we could see the pavement below.

We wasted a therapy session while Jon whined about the embarrassment of riding in Mom's sixty-two-fifty, which, according to Jon, was a clear indicator to anyone within twenty miles that he was a foster kid. Only an impoverished foster parent would drive such a piece of junk. He insisted our therapist take a field trip to the parking lot to inspect the car. When Tim agreed that it was a piece of junk, I was amused, and Jon felt vindicated – until Tim spent the rest of the session reminding Jon that even pieces of junk have proper owners and he owed me restitution for the damage. The car wasn't worth repair, so instead, Jon negotiated to prepare a Caution sign for the dashboard which warned Hole in Floor. Furthermore, since he wouldn't want anyone else to be harmed by his actions, he would be designated shotgun rider. Yep, he would ALWAYS be the one riding in the front passenger seat – even when there was a choice to ride in the van. Jon made a memorable statement as he attempted to justify his action to Papa, "I'd rather have a car in the driveway that looks nice and doesn't run, than drive something that looks like that."

Tap Dancing on Quicksand While Gargling Peanut Butter

What Do I Have to Do?

There is a well-known foster child syndrome: "What do I have to do to make you, too, reject me?"

In preparation for fostering teenagers who have been adjudicated delinquent[1], one may choose to pack away those breakable heirlooms that are irreplaceable. Pawnable gold or diamond jewelry pieces can be placed in a safe deposit box or stored with a relative. Unused checks may need to be locked up. It usually only takes about two weeks to dispel the myth that teenagers "just need love."

It was a lesson I learned the hard way. My gold nugget initial charm, herringbone chains, even one diamond ring are gone because we couldn't find the pawn shop which bought them.

By the way, for those foster parents or parents of addicts who are reading this, pawn shops will usually cooperate with you. On more than one occasion, we have been able to retrieve the pawned item for the price of the ticket. The other alternative is to press charges on your child. If you do so, the police will hold the pawned item for 120 days as evidence while they investigate the case. Then it is returned to you at no charge and the pawn broker loses his loan. It's your choice.

Because foster children have faced rejection after rejection, it is wise to take steps toward providing a fail-safe environment. Remember, biological parents have disappeared from their daily lives, and it takes time to establish visitation—sometimes years to achieve reunification. Sometimes reunification is never a possibility, and a child can spend years going from foster home to foster home. The assigned social worker changes too often. A child can have two or even three social workers in one year. The tendency to "blow out" of a foster family is common-place. For some foster children, it is less painful to control the failure of a placement, than face the fear of rejection.

Jon's first three months with us were troublesome, yet his attempts at achieving rejection were mild compared to most foster kids. He simply set up pandemonium.

There is one hilariously dysfunctional day I'd like to share with you. First, however, I'd like to give you some background data on James Ed, Kenny, Larry, and Tim.

---

[1] Adjudicated Delinquent refers to any teen less than 16 years of age and over 6 years of age who has committed a crime or infraction and has been proven guilty in a court of law.

James Ed

James Ed was only five years old when he was dropped off at the infamous Broadview Center in Cleveland, Ohio, that warehoused the most extreme cases of disabled children. There was a new baby at home and Mom couldn't handle James's hyperactivity.

When his tests revealed a normal IQ range, with no explanation for his rambunctious behavior, his parents refused to pick him up. Unfortunately for James, his only malady was hyperactivity and his ultimate misfortune was being ADHD before it was diagnosable. There was no appropriate placement for this little boy in 1969. When no place was found for him, and his parents still refused to receive him, an eleven-year travesty began. He was trapped – a normal, over-active, adorable little boy amid grossly deformed, developmentally non-functional children: children he could not communicate with, relate to, or play with. He became a junior care-giver at the ripe old age of five.

James was fifteen when a new Special Education teacher was hired. He quickly bonded with this wonderful woman who decried warehousing and believed that Developmentally Delayed children could learn. As she began working with James, she became painfully aware that he did not belong at Broadview Center. She contacted a prominent children's rights attorney.

Meanwhile James began memorizing the phone numbers of state senators and congressmen. He stole a set of keys from a staff member and let himself into Administrative Offices during the night. He dialed number after number, leaving the same message, "My name is James Ed. I am in Broadview Center. I don't belong here. Okay? Get me out of here!" (I can still hear the twangy way James said "okay?")

After legislative intervention and legal action, we were invited to visit Broadview Center to meet James and consider becoming his foster parents. We signed in at the institution's front desk and were told to have a seat on a bench in the foyer while they fetched James. Papa excused himself to go to the Men's Room, leaving me there, alone, on the garden-style bench. Quickly, I became surrounded by children with malformed faces, drooling mouths, and exploring fingers. I was overwhelmed by the extreme physical and developmental disabilities of these precious children.

Suddenly, from behind this throng of a dozen crowding bodies, I heard a welcome voice, "Hey, you guys, move it, move it! This is MY mom!" He shushed the rocking, forgotten children away, turned to me with his outstretched hand and won my heart with his, "Hi! I'm James Ed and I'm gonna be your kid." We were only able to visit for a half hour, but that was all it took for us to make a commitment to become his foster parents.

As I walked to the car, the duality of images—severely DD children contrasted with James Ed and the realization of his eleven-year imprisonment in this drab institution churned my psyche and I vomited in the parking lot.

Two days later James joined our family, which within a month grew to five teenage boys, one-year-old Sierra and Mom and Dad.

****

James was our ramrod. He knew where everyone was at any given moment and what they were doing and reported it to every family member round-robin.

During the eleven years he lived at the Center, James was never allowed to answer the phone, make Kool-Aid, put a pizza in the oven, drink soda, have all the cereal he wanted or spend a moment in solitude. We had the joy of experiencing many firsts with him. Our household consumption of dry cereal quadrupled immediately after his arrival.

The most important new opportunity for James was the privilege of answering the phone. This was still the era when most middle-class homes had only one phone – on the wall in the kitchen. Our house was a typical Archie Bunker house with a finished basement, giving us three floors of living space. When the phone rang it became routine for everyone to flatten themselves on a wall, slam themselves into a chair or climb onto a sofa – to get out of any area between James' whereabouts and the phone. It was a wonder to behold. James made a miraculous metamorphosis into Road Runner. The other boys would make sound effects as good as the cartoons as James made it to the phone by the second ring no matter where he had been. He would pause for a quick breath; snap his neck for effect and answer, "Pennington's, James speaking." Yep, if I was in the kitchen doing dishes or cooking dinner, I learned quickly NOT to answer the phone. It only took one collision with Road Runner to learn my lesson. James could get there faster than I could cross the room.

Sarah ala Bo Derek, James Ed, and Sierra Danielle

The braids were a cosmetology project of Kenny's

Tap Dancing on Quicksand While Gargling Peanut Butter
Kenny

Ohio State Law did not allow foster parents to "search" the rooms of foster children. If we suspected the existence of contraband of any kind we had to call the probation officer or social worker who could then instigate a search.

One day, I was putting laundry away in the boys' rooms while two-year-old Sierra played on the floor. Underneath Kenny's bed, she found a hand towel rolled up neatly. She pulled it out and brought it to me, "Look, Mommy, dirty." Bless her. She thought it was dirty laundry and I honored her by putting it in the now-empty laundry basket. As soon as I put Sierra down for her nap, I ran back to check the contents of the towel. I was not surprised to find a bag of cheap Colombian marijuana. I called Kenny's case worker and together we hatched a plan which would teach Kenny a lesson while avoiding legal action.

Papa and I had a great time flushing the pot down the toilet and refilling the bag with dirty broom straw, whole cloves, parsley – you get my drift. We carefully rolled the bag into the towel and placed it back under Kenny's bed. We made a pact to say nothing to anyone.

The windows to the boys' two bedrooms faced the front of the house which had a flat surface just outside the windows affording an excellent place for the boys to congregate and talk junk and obviously smoke pot out of our earshot and sense of smell. However, Papa and I had relinquished our bedroom during my mother's visit and were sleeping in the extra bedroom in the basement. From that vantage point we could hear and smell everything.

In the middle of the night, Papa and I were awakened by *expletives deleted* as Kenny demanded furiously to know who had ripped off his stash!!

Sarah Pennington

No one knew who did the dastardly deed and no one confessed. Ah! 'Twas the fulfillment of a disciplinary dream.

Tap Dancing on Quicksand While Gargling Peanut Butter

Larry

Larry was a buff, young-punk Marlon Brando type. He was also a blatant pothead. He was thrilled when Santa brought him a weight set for Christmas and loved showing off his biceps. He also enjoyed showing off other buff body parts. When I had our Christmas pictures developed, I discovered a close-up of his most organic part. He was furious when I ripped it up and destroyed the negative.

I wasn't surprised, then, when we received a call from the high school informing us that Larry had been exposing himself on the school grounds for $5.00 a peek. The boy had made $75.00 and was angry when I confiscated it from the zipper pouch in his baseball cap and made him put the money in the offering plate at church the next Sunday.

Larry enjoyed "sex talk" with the others boys, was openly bi-sexual and braggadocios about his sexual exploits.

****

A Texas newspaper carried Larry's obituary in 1993. It read, "He died after a long illness." He was thirty-one.

Sarah Pennington

Tim

I have no photos of Tim. He had an affinity for white shirts, had short dirty-blonde hair, and looked like a miniature Southern Baptist preacher. He has remained in my heart and my prayers and has been burned into my psyche for almost thirty years now. Soon after he left us, I wrote the following account. It was based on the talks Tim and I had, the passages he shared with me from the 'Timothy Bible,' and information I gleaned from his grandmother.

****

Twelve-year-old Tim descended the basement stairs. He didn't like the damp coldness or the dark -- especially not the dark that let creepy things float in the air and made the imagination wild with the anticipation of something touching you in the night. He felt a cruel shove and heard his father's voice, deep and intimidating ordering him down, down, down the basement stairs.

Roughly prodded from behind, he crossed the pitch-black room, his arms reaching out before him, until his knee found the solitary metal chair his father had prepared for him. Tim sat gingerly on the edge of the chair and waited.

Leaving the boy instructions to memorize scripture, his father lit a candle, admonishing him, "If you waste time, you'll run out of light."

Watching his father ascend the stairs, he wanted to cry out, to beg him not to leave him, but in fear he clutched himself about the middle and wept silent tears.

"Thy word is a lamp unto my feet." [What is that noise, that chittering near my left foot – oh please let me out of here] "and a light unto my path" [I must remember, I must. The candle is burning down. He'll be back and I won't know the verse and he'll beat me. Please let me remember.]

Looking toward the stairway, the candle gone, the darkness enveloping, he thought he saw figures, shapes, movement. No it couldn't be. There was nothing in that black hole but himself and he knew it.

What had he done that had been so bad? The guys at school talked about it. They all touched themselves there. What was so bad? He still felt the red-hot burn, where his father had held his penis under the scalding spray of the shower. Why had he done that? [Wish Grandma was here. She'd put salve there and make it feel better.] Maybe he could go stay with Grandma for a while. Maybe…

Tap Dancing on Quicksand While Gargling Peanut Butter

The door opened and a shaft of light filtered down the stairway. He trembled, knowing he would be told to recite. "Please God, if only I can say the verse correctly, I will get out of this basement."

[Think about Grandma. Think, Tim, think about Gram. You don't have to be here.] Were there voices? Were they only in his head? Grandma baking cookies. Tollhouse cookies, his favorite. He didn't feel the brutal blows to his stomach, nor hear the harsh words. He mumbled, but could not hear his own sound.

As the man ascended the stairs, he left the voices behind him saying, "In the morning, in the morning, in the morning." [Does he plan to leave me here all night in the dark with the voices?]

Tim wanted to cry out but there were no words, no sound, only darkness.

Soon he would lose track of the days and nights. It was dark – so dark – and the candle never lasted long enough. The verses ran together. [Why am I an abomination to God? What did I do? What does queer mean?]

Somewhere into the second week in the basement, hungry and weak, Tim mustered the courage to ask for Grandma, to ask to go to Grandma's. "Maybe," he said, "I could memorize better there."

"Dead." That's what his father had said, "Your Grandma is dead."

Then I must be an abomination to God, he thought. He took Grandma away. Soon Tim began to embrace the voices, the voices out of the darkness that would never go away.

****

Tim was only with us for two weeks. He spent his time sitting on the floor in a corner of our dining room, working on the Timothy Bible, twisting the scriptures angrily to anti-Christianity. He freaked the boys out as he argued with the voices in his head, so they avoided him as much as possible.

He would come to the foot of our bed during the night begging to sleep with us – afraid of the demons he believed were coming to take him away. We could not allow him into our bed, of course, so I would make a place for him just outside the open door of our bedroom and sit with him until he fell asleep.

We were blessed to facilitate a reunion with his grandmother. When she walked in the door, he became hysterical and needed reassurance that she was, indeed, alive and well and loved him very much.

Tim was part of our mix just long enough for a bed to become available in the teen psychiatric unit of a state hospital.

Sarah Pennington

The Set-Up for Pandemonium

Now that you know all the boys, let me introduce you to my mother and tell you about the day Jon Michael set up pandemonium.

My mother, whom the boys called Miss Gladys, came to visit for three months during the spring and summer of 1980. Mother was a genteel Southern belle, a pastor's wife for 37 years, who possessed a spiritual wisdom that blessed us all. She was also down to earth. She knew when to jump in with all four feet and when to "mind my own bizzniss." So the day Jon 'set up' the other four boys, she retreated to the upstairs and watched and listened from a bedroom window amazed and amused at Jon's skillful creation of pandemonium

As the youngest of a family of nine children for his first fifteen years, Jon had become a master manipulator when it came to setting up conflict, disengaging himself and watching the resulting chaos with an appearance of total innocence.

Jon began with James. "Kenny said he's sick and tired of you slamming into him when he's trying to answer the phone. He says you're a retard."

To Kenny, Jon reported, "Larry is the one who smoked your stash. I saw him!"

Hurriedly, he cornered Larry and said, "That crazy Tim said he's putting a spell on you 'cause you're evil and perverted!"

Finally, to Tim, Jon said, "I just heard Kenny, Larry and James talking about you. They said you're crazy, dude."

Even in those days of his greatest dysfunction, Jon consistently charmed middle-aged women. It was inevitable that Jon, wisely, hauled butt across the street to the safety of the middle-aged female clerk at our neighborhood store and gleefully involved her in watching the action, which went something like this:

James confronted Kenny, "Hey, queer, whaddya mean calling me a retard? I'm not a retard, I'm normal and I'll answer the phone if I want to."

Kenny defended himself, "Listen, retard, I never called you a retard and where do you get off calling me queer....Who told you I called you a retard?"

"Jon."

Irked, Kenny found Larry. "Hey, Larry, you owe me man! That was good stash. You better pay me for it!"

Larry smirked, "I never took your stash, dude. "Besides," he bluffed, "who do you think you're talking to? I know good weed and that was cheap

Tap Dancing on Quicksand While Gargling Peanut Butter

stuff, man, had big pods in it, thick and dry like broom straw! I never took your cheap smoke, dude! Who told you I smoked it?"

"Jon."

"Anyway, Larry continued, "I got worse problems than you. That crazy psycho-Satanist, Tim, is putting a spell on me. Probably gonna shrink my pecker!"

"Oh, good grief," Kenny blurted, "who told you that?"

"Jon."

Tim appeared from around a corner and gloated, "You think I can shrink your pecker? Well, I can, you know. Besides, the Timothy Bible says, 'Peckers are an abomination to the Lord.' Matter of fact, dude, you are an abomination to me. Where do you guys get off calling me crazy? You're the ones getting all riled up over that stupid, blabbermouth, Jon."

Kenny was defensive. "Hey! We never called you crazy, man."

Macho Larry was scared. "Please don't shrink my pecker."

In unison, Kenny and Larry queried, "Who said we called you crazy?"

"Jon."

"Jon! Where are you? We're gonna kick your..."

Right on cue, a neighborhood police car pulled up to our place with lights flashing.[2]

Four boys shut up, dispersed to the front steps and sat down quietly.

Kenny took the lead. "Wha—what's the matter officer?"

"Your mom just called and said I should check on her place, that there might be a fight going on."

Behind the officer, Jon Michael miraculously appeared, peeping around the policeman in feigned horror.

"They were gonna kick my...."

"Yeah, your mom said you probably set up the whole fight."

"How'd she know...?"

While the store clerk sent Jon to the freezer to fill the milk shelves, she had called me. Now, she looked skyward to the upstairs window where my mother, (who had called me and stayed on hold while I called 911), gave the clerk a smile and a wave.

---

[2] Our foster parent group had done citizen ride-alongs with our neighborhood police, who noted our locations and became available 24/7 to assist us. Thank you Officer David Young.

Sarah Pennington

The officer waited until I arrived and stayed long enough for me to give a week's grounding to four boys for fighting and talking each other down. Jon, on the other hand, received Shadow Detail – a fate the boys detested. Except for bathroom time, he spent every waking minute in the presence of Papa or me for the following week.

Jon was easy. It only took this one incident to cure him of instigating, agitating, trouble-making pandemonium. In his mind, this was the worst he could dish out, and we weren't going to reject him — only pull him closer.

At sixteen, Jon asked us to adopt him. We could not. His mother, after years of horrible abuse and several stays in psychiatric wards, had left his father and begun a new life with a new husband and her tenth child. She was gratefully willing to do anything for Jon, including signing relinquishment papers. His father, however, stated, "That little bastard ain't coming back here and I ain't signing no papers."

Miss Gladys had the wisdom to cry with Jon and remind him that he would always have us – and eight siblings who would always want to know him – eight siblings who carried the same birth-name.

While we would never be able to formally adopt Jon, he became permanently *ours*.

By the time Miss Gladys went home to Georgia, she agreed, "Jon is a keeper."

Miss Gladys, Church Mother

The three months Mama spent with us that year afforded me precious memories, chief of which was watching my mama become the Church Mother of a predominantly Black church.

John and Addie Adams pastored Church of Tomorrow in Jesus Christ, a small predominantly African American congregation where our obnoxious family was welcome. The Adams also fostered teenage boys, so Pastor John designated Papa to keep an eye on both the Adams and Pennington boys as well as any thievable items during the service.

I didn't know how my mother would respond to our church. Alabama and Georgia in the 1980's were not far removed from the Alabama and Georgia of the 1960's. While Blacks and Whites now mixed well in the workplace, they did not socialize or visit each other's homes. That was my generation, but Mama was from the prior generation where my Aunt had a seventy-year-old Black man she referred to as "my yard boy." She would offer him ice water in a fruit jar, he would graciously kowtow, "Thank you, Miss Mahgrit" and then watch her throw the jar away. This was the South where I was raised in the George C. Wallace White Way (taken from the white-asphalt highway which traversed the state of Alabama.) This was the South which created my mother, a sixty-six-year-old woman who was visibly nervous her first Sunday at Church of Tomorrow in Jesus Christ.

Addie Adams quickly put Mama at ease and they became Sisters in the Lord, talking on the phone every day, praying over our boys. It was a time of racial healing for my mother.

Those daily prayer calls were also the source of my sixteen-year consistent prayer, "Lord whatever it takes, please bring Jon back to you."

The second Sunday Mama was at the black church, our treasurer, a well-dressed-well-blessed, red-haired teacher in her fifties requested permission to speak. "Church," she began in her refined voice, "I have consistently maintained that I am too young to be the Church Mother. I respectfully request to defer to Miss Gladys during her tenure with us."

Mama was brought to the altar and with tears streaming down her face, she welcomed embraces, kisses on the check and "I love you, Mother" from the congregation in which we were the only white family. Oh my soul – to see my Mama honored, blessed, and healed.

Three months later, at the end of her visit with us, she was asked to say a few words on her last Sunday at church. She mentioned the humor she found in watching her lily-white daughter direct an all-Black choir. It was, indeed, humorous. We would get to the end of the special music. I would flap my chubby arms high in the air and perform an exquisite cut-off signal. The choir, obviously filled with the Spirit, would continue singing. (I love that about African American church choirs – they sing until the Spirit says to stop.) Sunday after Sunday, I'd give the cut off signal, then walk around to the alto section and join in. I loved seeing Mama's eyes twinkle as we exchanged a glance. As Mother shared her heart, she thanked the congregation for loving her and requested Addie and I sing Andre Crouch's "Soon and Very Soon" for her one more time.

The next day, I drove her to my brother's home in Georgia. Somewhere in Kentucky, she asked me to pull over. She told me how much the past months had meant to her, how proud she was of me and what an honor it had been to be the Church Mother of Church of Tomorrow in Jesus Christ. Then she paused for effect…"But, if you EVER tell ANYONE in our family about me being the Church Mother in a Black church I'll never speak to you again! I still have to live with them you know."

"Mother! I would never betray your confidence!"

"Yes, you would."

"Okay, I would…but I won't. I promise."

The next year Gladys' friend, Addie battled cancer. Early one morning Pastor John called to tell me, "Miss Addie has gone on to Glory. Would you call Mother Gladys for me?" I prayed with my pastor and composed myself before making the call.

I began, "Hi, Mama, how are you this morning?"

"You're calling to tell me Miss Addie has gone to Heaven."

"How'd you know?"

"While I was in the shower this morning, I heard her singing "Soon and Very Soon," and the next thing I knew I was singing it with her and I could

Tap Dancing on Quicksand While Gargling Peanut Butter

remember all the words. You know I never learned them. Did she go peacefully?"

"Yes, Mama, in her sleep."

Addie's passing closed that chapter in my mother's life, but for better or worse, she remained involved – from a distance – in Jon's life.

I'm Not Goin' Anywhere!

One of Mother's wisdom-talks with Papa and me that summer was about giving two-year-old, Sierra, a peaceful, stable home environment. We agreed with her and made the decision to rotate out of foster care and focus on adoption. We waited for the right time to share this information with our foster sons.

Every Saturday we had a family meeting to discuss the boys' accomplishments; school, clothing, and financial needs; disciplinary complaints and sibling issues.

Papa covered the issues each boy had placed on the agenda, praised the noted accomplishments and then turned the meeting over to me saying, "Mom has something important to talk to you about."

It didn't matter that the first thing out of my mouth was, "First of all, each of you will remain with us as long as you need to." The moment the words, "We are no longer going to foster parent" came out of my mouth, Jon Michael became hysterical.

"I'm not going anywhere. I'm gonna live here 'til I'm forty. You can't make me leave!"

Little Sierra hopped into his lap, threw choking arms around his neck, pleading, "Don't cry Bubby, don't cry!" The three other boys crowded around him consoling,

"They already said you can stay, stupid," chimed in James.

"Boys, don't say stupid," I responded.

"Well, he is stupid. Shoot, I'd have already thrown his sorry butt out!"

"James Edward!"

Jon whined, "I can stay?"

"Until Hell freezes over," I promised.

Jon returned his baby sister's hug, complaining, "Sierra, you're choking me. Stop kissing me. You're slobbering on me."

"I love you, Bubby," she giggled.

"I love you too, Little Bit."

As each young man turned eighteen and moved on, Jon remained, until a juvenile court judge told him he must live on his own for thirty days before being released from probation.

Tap Dancing on Quicksand While Gargling Peanut Butter

Jon stood up and said, "Respectfully sir, I waited until I was fifteen to have a Mom and a Dad, so emotionally I'm only three-years-old and I still need my parents. I've worked and saved the money for my apartment, so if I have to live on my own for thirty days I will. BUT, as soon as you release me, I'm going home to my Mama."

And he did.

Sarah Pennington

For This One Who Doesn't Believe in You...

It was perfect timing when Dan took a job in Chicken, Alaska. Jon had been on his own for thirty days and when I called to give him the news that we'd be moving, it only took him two days to appear on our doorstep packed and ready to go. "I've sold my bike and my stereo and I have my own money. You're not leaving me. I'm going with you!"

Off we went in a little brown Capri with luggage on the roof, in the trunk, and one bag in the tiny back seat with Sierra's car seat. Jon and I took turns sardine-ing in the back seat and cramping-up in the front bucket.

We arrived in Anchorage in time for dinner at our friends' where, exhausted, we slept on bean bags in their den for two nights. We found an apartment on the second morning, put away the contents of our meager boxes and sent Papa off to Chicken by helicopter.

Within forty-eight hours Jon Michael had a job -- as a detailer at a Bavarian Motors. Sierra began making neighborhood friends and I busied myself with settling into a tiny two-bedroom apartment.

A week before we would receive both Jon and Papa's first pay checks, I realized we were in trouble. I had the fixings for a healthy dinner. Breakfast would consist of flour and water pancakes and brown sugar syrup. There was one glass of milk for Sierra and enough coffee for a half-pot of brew for Jon and me.

Jon was frantic. "Call somebody, Mom. Go to the Food Bank, call some churches. You lived here before. Call some old friends." I smiled and told him God would take care of us. This, of course, only angered this young man who had been so hurt by "church people."

I went to my room that Friday night and, leaving the door open, got down on my knees beside my bed and began to pray. "Lord, for this young one who doesn't believe in You, can you please provide us with enough food 'til payday?"

At 10 a.m. on Saturday morning there was a knock on the door. There stood Macon Roberts, a tall, African American probation officer, with a big grin on his face.

Macon had been the probation officer for several of our foster sons prior to our two-year stay in Ohio and I adored him.

With a helper, Macon began bringing in box after box of food, dry goods, frozen venison, halibut, and store-bought meat. As he helped me put things away, Macon realized my cupboards had been empty and shook his head and smiled ear to ear.

Tap Dancing on Quicksand While Gargling Peanut Butter

"How did you know?" I asked.

"I didn't. We were just sitting around talking about ya'll being back in town and wondering how soon you'd be ready to take some more boys. Someone said we ought to do something nice for you and I suggested we give you a pounding. You know these Alaskans didn't have a clue what I was talking about 'til I explained it was pound-goods of groceries."

As Jon, speechless, helped Macon bring box after box of groceries into the apartment, I filled every cabinet, the refrigerator, the freezer and the counters.

Thanks, Macon!

Thank You, Lord!

Sarah Pennington

I'm gay

We were all ecstatic when Papa joined us again and reveled in the stories he had to tell. Our favorite was his telling of the night he went to the outhouse and a little bear came to explore the delightful scent. Baby Bear propped his paws up on the door, trapping Papa there for what seemed like hours, until Mama Bear finally called her baby and he went away. Little Sierra would ask Papa to re-live his misfortune many times, always mimicking her daddy peeking out the outhouse door until he was sure Mama Bear was far, far away.

Sometime that summer, Jon had told me he was gay. He wanted me to tell his dad, but I refused, reminding him that something this important was his news to share.

For two weeks I watched Jon pace the floor every evening trying to get up the nerve to talk to his dad. I hurt so much for him and tried to wait it out.

Finally, I couldn't stand it any longer. As I cleared the dinner dishes I reminded Jon in front of his dad that the two of them had something to talk about. I eased myself out of the room, but remained in hearing distance. There was an eternity of silence before Jon blurted out, "Okay, Dad, I need to tell you something." There was another long pause before he exhaled, "I'm gay."

Again, an eternity of silence. Then I heard the most poignant words I will ever hear my Marine speak. Four excruciatingly beautiful words:

"Son, I love you."

Jon and Sierra

That first summer in Alaska, Bubby and two-year-old Sierra's relationship was a wonder to behold. 'If Mommy says no, ask Bubby' became her motto. After all Grandma was too far away. When I said no to the new $35.00 Barbie car, Jon bought it anyway. While I would be irritated for a moment, I cherished their sibling bonding.

Although Macon's 'pounding' had given Jon an excellent example of God's provision for His children, he still wasn't eager to attend church and his profession of his gay lifestyle placed another wedge between him and the church door.

Each time Sierra was in a children's program, he would sneak into the back and sit in the last row, staying only long enough to see her performance. I only knew he was there because Sierra would wave and mouth, "Hi, Bubby."

Her big brother – her knight in shining armor—was priceless to her.

Jon Michael, the Man

Jon was an extraordinary man-son. He lived at home until he was twenty-two. He never failed to call if he would be out late or staying overnight elsewhere.

After he was on his own, he'd come home while I was at work, clean the house top to bottom and leave a note on the fridge, "I love you Mom." He'd show up on the weekend to do the yard work, wash the cars or do projects with Dad.

When he was twenty-one, Jon confessed to us that he was a cross-dresser. He invited us to meet his alter-ego, Brandy, at a hotel coffee shop which looked out over the lobby of the Anchorage Sheraton.

We found a table near the lobby where we would have a clear view and ordered coffee. We were both nervous and almost hoping he wouldn't show. He did appear, however, gloriously and confidently. I was breathless as I watched a beautiful, graceful 'woman' walk across the lobby to the lounge amidst a gaggle of clumsy men-dressed-as-women. 'She' stopped, turned and made eye-contact. I was heart-broken and amazed. Only a Tyra Banks could have walked as gracefully in six-inch sequined heels. 'She' wore her own hair, one side held back by a barrette. 'Her' make-up was impeccable. 'Her' posture and walk was alluringly feminine. If I had not known that Brandy was really Jon Michael....

It wasn't until we got home that it hit me like a sledge-hammer. What if some guy picked-up 'Brandy' thinking he really was female and then found out....

Within weeks the papers carried a story of a murder that hit too close to home – a young cross-dresser picked up by a gentleman who believed he was picking up a woman. The gentleman, in anger and embarrassment, grabbed a kitchen knife and stabbed the victim, who was pronounced dead on the scene. It scared me to death. Still, it did not deter Jon or his friends from their weekends of playing dress-up.

For the next ten years, I would worry about this part of his life and wake in the night and pray.

Tap Dancing on Quicksand While Gargling Peanut Butter

Free Tickets

For a shy guy, Jon was adept at making good, loyal friends. One benefit of his circle of friends was all the free tickets we received to local venues featuring artists like Willie Nelson, Bill Cosby, and John Denver.

One Anchorage hotel hosted a dinner theatre and Jon gave us tickets to an Alaska-themed musical. We were seated at a classy table with exquisite linens and candlelight. We feasted on sourdough bread, halibut and steamed veggies. Dessert was Papa's favorite, cherry cheesecake.

A young man, one of Jon's friends, came to our table and greeted us. He motioned to a long table behind us and we waved at the long row of Jon's buddies – all gay men. Seated at the end of the table were two large, buxom blondes who we did not recognize.

The musical production began and all too soon it was intermission. We excused ourselves to go to the restrooms. I returned to our table and enjoyed my tea and waited for Papa. I was beginning to worry; it was almost time for the curtain when Papa came huffing to the table.

I asked, "Are you okay? Where have you been?"

Grinning, Papa confessed, "You know that big blonde behind you? Well, I got to the men's room and she went in right in front of me. I wasn't going in there!"

"What did you do?"

"I went across the street to the Tesoro station!"

After the show, the big, beautiful blonde came to our table. The moment he opened his mouth, we knew it was Jon's best friend -- a large robust man we called Little John.

Sarah Pennington

This is Jon's Muthuh

Between 1980 and 1989, we adopted fourteen-year-old Stephanie Michelle in Alaska, moved to Georgia and adopted newborn Jonathan Israel and finally migrated to Washington State. The years were full and blessed.

In the fall of 1991, I flew to Anchorage with three agendas: to sing at a friend's wedding, meet my first grandchild, and get to know Ed, Jon's partner.

All went well until Ed did not show up for dinner.

Ed, Mama, and Jon

This was the era when families disowned their gay children. Ed's parents had devastated him by throwing his clothing out on the front lawn when they discovered he was gay. All he knew about us was that we were 'churchy'. He was terrified of meeting me.

I am a stubborn, bull-headed woman – especially when it comes to the well-being of my children. So, I told Jon if the mountain wouldn't come to Mama, Mama would go to the mountain. That meant I would have my first encounter with a gay bar.

Just before eleven p.m., Jon and I arrived at the Jade room, an upscale lounge for gays and lesbians. There was a bar, a dance floor, and a small alcove where we could sit out of the way and wait for Ed. Jon's friends came over to say hello, give hugs and make me feel welcome. I was treated with honor and respect. When a couple of lesbian women started toward our table, however, Jon's friend, Cedrick, appointed himself to be my bodyguard. A six-foot-plus African American dressed in six-inch heels, a beautiful caftan and a long wig, he elongated his gargantuan arms and four-inch fingernails before me announcing, "This is Jon's muthah!"

"Cedrick," I protested, "I'm okay."

Tap Dancing on Quicksand While Gargling Peanut Butter

He laughed, "I don't want them to scare off the church lady, dahlin'!"

With all the hoopla, we almost missed Ed's entrance, but there he stood, handsome and debonair. He searched for Jon, saw me sitting there and almost walked back out the door. I stood, and approached him in front of a bar full of expectant eyes. I held out my arms, drew him to me and hugged him tightly. We spent the evening and into the early morning hours becoming family and I left the Jade Room with a peace, knowing that Ed would now be comfortable coming to our home.

During my week in Alaska, the three of us had two more dates. We went to dinner one evening and spent a Saturday shopping. I went home with a new wardrobe courtesy of Jon and Ed.

Sarah Pennington

Weebok and Night Sweats

The summer of 1992, we flew to Georgia to visit Mama (Miss Gladys). While I was there she sold me Old Betsy, a 1973 top-of-the-line Ford Humongous, for a dollar. Mama set a great example for her children by making the decision on her own to relinquish her car before we would have to take it from her. She knew she was going blind. We did not. "No sense troublin' you," she'd say later. We were proud of the vintage, well-kept monstrosity and piled in to make the trip back to Washington State via Texas.

Jon was twenty-nine when we visited him in Texas, where he—without a high school diploma or a GED—had become the Parts Manager of a Bavarian Motors in Dallas/Ft. Worth.

We were immediately concerned when we saw Jon. He had lost a lot of weight, the Belle's Palsy[3], which is noticeable in the picture from my visit in 1991, had not gone away.

Papa and I had read everything we could get our hands on about HIV/AIDS and knew what we were looking at—he showed all the symptoms of full-blown AIDS. He had night sweats, sores and bruises on his legs that would not heal, the Belle's Palsy, a persistent cough, and complained of joint pain. We encouraged him to get tested to no avail. Jon persisted, "I don't want to know 'til I have to."

We chose to enjoy the boys for the rest of the visit and try not to worry.

While the guys both had good jobs, they had a side business selling Dalmatians. Their two Dalmatians, Reebok and Noelle were beautiful, mischievous and made our visit quite entertaining. There was a precious bonus: Weebok.

Noelle was unfaithful to Reebok and had a fling with a terrier that had jumped the fence. The resulting litter consisted of several puppies that looked totally Dalmatian and were sold as dummy Dalmatians (the buyer knows they are not register-able and doesn't care). The runt of the litter had the markings of a Dalmatian and the Dr. Spock ears of a terrier. She was adorable. Noelle rejected her, so Jon Michael fed her baby formula and baby cereal around the clock. Sierra and Jonathan were thrilled when he gifted them with the puppy.

On the second day of our visit, Jon asked Papa if they could prime and paint Old Betsy. Her leather interior was immaculate, but the outside showed

---

[3] Belle's palsy is a partial paralysis of the face.

Tap Dancing on Quicksand While Gargling Peanut Butter

her age with a few nicks and scrapes. While they papered and painted, Sierra and Nicholas played happily with the dogs. Ed asked me to go for a drive.

As he drove me around the scenic area, pointing out celebrity homes, including the compound of Martina Navratilova, Ed poured his heart out. "Mom, I'm so worried. Jon won't get tested. He's such a big chicken. If he'd get tested he could get on medication."

"I know. If he waits too late, it will go quickly and we'll lose him," I acknowledged. I also urged Ed, though symptom free, to be tested as well.

"I've already told him we'd go together." Ed pleaded, "Would you talk to him before you go? Just see if you can get through to him?"

Finally, on the day we were leaving, Jon and I went into his bedroom, shut the door for privacy, and talked. I cried and begged him to get tested.

We made the drive back to Washington, mine and Papa's hearts breaking while forcing a happy face for fourteen-year-old Sierra and three-year-old Jonathan.

A few days after our return I received a call from Ed. Yes, Jon had been tested — they both had — and now we'd have to wait three weeks for the results.

We knew what Jon's results would be. That didn't make it any easier when we got the news.

"Do you want the good news or the bad news first?" Jon asked.

"Good news."

"Ed doesn't have HIV."

"Awesome – and you?"

"I only have 11 T-cells, Mom."

"What does that mean, son?"

"I should have 1200 T-cells. I only have 11. It means I'm outta here. I have full-blown AIDS."

During that call and the many that would follow, we talked about his options, which always included coming home. Jon was consistent, he would live as normally as possible for as long as possible. He made it clear that he would not come home until he knew he was dying, because after all that is what coming home meant.

September, 1993
Driving in the Rain

Moose season in Alaska is always tempting for Papa. When our ex-son-in-law invited him to join a hunt, he couldn't resist. It was important for him to go, to have this time away in the tundra to think. We knew it was inevitable that we would receive the dreaded call soon that it was time for Jon to come home to die. But not tonight.

Tonight I was driving after midnight to SeaTac Airport, looking forward to seeing my husband and hearing his stories of the successful moose hunt and the antics of our Alaska grandbabies.

The windshield wipers were fighting a losing battle with torrents of raindrops. The salty tears streaming down my face were smaller, bitterer. All the pus-laden, putrid emotions of the past year came to a head like a boil ready to explode.

There was no one to hear me. The torrential rain shrouded my car with privacy as I cried out to God, "Why, God, why? Why do I have to watch my husband come in from the woods with his eyes swollen from crying – trying to hide his pain and tears from me to protect me?"

"Because I love you."

"Why do I have to see my 14-year-old, Sierra, get off the school bus angry and run in the door in tears, because boys on the bus are cracking gay jokes? You don't have a clue what that feels like. Why do I have to go through this?"

"Because I chose you."

"How can I explain to my 5-year-old, Jonathan, the brother he adores is going to leave him? How do I explain death and AIDS to a little child?"

"I will give you the words."

"You know what angers me the most, don't you? You promised me that You would comfort me in all things that I might comfort others. Well, God, where is the parent who's supposed to be walking this with me?"

"Sarah, I'm right here. People said my Son deserved to die. I was there with his mother as she knelt before the cross. I was there with his earthly father as he, too, wept bitter tears. I was there when his brothers and sisters were taunted by other children. And you say I don't have a clue?!"

Humbled, I replied, "I'm sorry."

"I will walk through this with you and when you cannot go on......then I will carry you."

Tap Dancing on Quicksand While Gargling Peanut Butter

October, 1993
We Can't Walk This with You

Papa returned from his moose hunt, refreshed, and full of stories about the bear he'd seen, his terrifically terrifying novice excursions on the four-wheelers trying to keep up with the other hunters who were expert quad drivers.

His time in the Alaskan wilderness had given Papa the time alone he needed with his Heavenly Father and he came back to me stronger, wiser. He said, "It won't be easy, honey, but it will be worth it."

Hindsight is 20/20. Today we can see clearly that it was God's plan for us to walk our AIDS Journey in the Christian community. Dan and I are both preachers' kids. We grew up 'walking through the fire' of this world. God knew we could take the rejection of friends, church and family and stand in the gap for our son. At the time, however, there were many things we did not understand.

We had been members of our church for four years. We had taught the Adult Singles; I sang in the choir, participated in drama, sang in a women's group, and sang solos.

Our county AIDS Coordinator offered to teach a Saturday class to members of our church who would like to support us once Jon came home. We presented the offer to our pastor.

We were not prepared for his response. With our family deacon standing beside him he admonished, "We can't support this! If you bring a homosexual into your home, you'll be condoning his sin and we cannot stand beside you in that decision. Have you considered the threat of infection[4] you'd be bringing to the church family? [5]

In dismay, we quietly collected our teenager and toddler and left the church, knowing we could not walk this journey alone, and with no clue what we were going to do.

After crying myself to sleep in my husband's strong arms, I slept a restless sleep. When I awoke the next morning, I collected myself, got Papa off to work, put Sierra on the bus for school and dressed little Jonathan for our outing to Mothers of Preschoolers (MOPS) at New Covenant Fellowship Foursquare Church.

---

[4] In 1993 the ways in which the HIV virus could be spread were still uncertain to the general public and many people were afraid of even secondary contact.

[5] During the next two years the President of the Southern Baptist Convention walked his own AIDS Journey and changed the hearts of many. I would return to this church to speak on AIDS.

Sarah Pennington

Jonathan and I had attended the MOPS program for three years. I was in my forties and since I also had grown children and MOPS had a need, I had been asked to be a Titus Woman for our group.[6] I spoke often, sang special music and loved the time I spent with the young civilian and Navy wives who attended with their little ones.

I took Jonathan to his Moppets class and started toward the sanctuary where I would present the devotion that morning. As I crossed the foyer, Pastor Tony called my name. "Sarah, I just came out of my prayer time. I've never proselytized in my whole life, but this morning God placed it on my heart to invite you and Dan (Papa) to New Covenant. He showed me that you are about to go through trial and we are the church that's supposed to walk through it with you."

"Even if it's AIDS?"

He paused only for a second, "Yes, Sarah, even if it's AIDS."

Wow! I didn't have time to talk, so I asked him to call Papa and told Pastor Tony I'd talk to him after MOPS.

For me it was one more scripture proven: God knows our need before we ask it [7]

The following Sunday we stepped into a new church family who treated us and our dilemma with respect and warmth. By the time Jon came home, everyone was aware, prepared and supportive.

---

[6] Titus 2:3 of the King James Bible requests that the older women teach the younger women how to love their husbands and children.

[7] Matthew 6:8

Tap Dancing on Quicksand While Gargling Peanut Butter

March, 1994

Come Get Him

Finally, the call came. Crying, Jon whined, "I have to come home and Ed won't come with me. Talk to him."

Ed came on the phone, his voice strained, "Mom, I can't handle it anymore. Jon is losing his mind. He's doing crazy things. He comes to my work and yells obscenities, accusing me of cheating on him. He even shouted yesterday that I was carrying HIV and was going to infect everybody! I almost got fired. He won't let me out of his sight for a second. He's not Jon anymore. Can you come get him?" He put Jon back on the phone.

"I want to keep my Audi. Can someone drive it for me? It's a little inconvenient with a GROSHONG[8] in my chest." His voice raised and lowered as he attempted to continue his argument with Ed.

I asked him why he was so upset. His response was delivered in typical Jon sarcasm. "I'm bleeding out of places I can't mention and it smells like old death. I have little places all over my body that look like someone injected water under the skin and they break open and scab over. I'm blind in one eye and the other is all blurry. I have psoriasis, and a mass is growing in my right lung. I can't sleep at night, because I have to get up and use the bathroom every hour and a half and the bathroom is down thirteen steps and my thighs and calves and the tops of my feet hurt severely when I have to climb back up the stairs. I have a hernia that wiggles every time I cough hard, and I've lost thirty pounds I can't gain back. I have a BOYFRIEND who is DESERTING me after I'VE GIVEN HIM EVERYTHING and you want to know why I'm upset!"

I told him we'd be there as soon as possible.

Papa decided that he would be the one to make the trip to Texas, made arrangements at work to take vacation and had me make a reservation with Greyhound, the cheapest travel option.

The following is Papa's account of what happened on their trip...

---

[8] A Groshong line, which can be left in for a long period, is common in terminal patients. The tip of the catheter is inserted into the superior vena cava, (a vein that carries blood from the upper half of the body into the heart), and then is tunneled under the skin to an incision in the chest wall, where the distal end exits the body. This allows syringes to provide medication through the tube, avoiding needle contact with the skin.

Sarah Pennington

I Wish I Had Hugged Him

It was a warm sunny day when I got on the Greyhound bus in Seattle. I felt relieved that the bus was not crowded and I had an empty row of seats in front and back of me. I wanted the freedom to think and reflect on what I had just agreed to do without making small talk with a stranger.

Bringing a gay, HIV-infected foster son to my home with two children was not a popular decision in our community, social or church circles and I had approximately fifteen hours to resolve all my internal turmoil about Jon and the situation. Was he a foster son or an adopted son? To my wife it was clear, he was her son - foster or adopted did not enter into her vocabulary or thoughts. To me there was a distinction in my mind and heart.

When we were at home with Jon there was no stress or distinction that had to be made about him being gay. However when we were away from home I was aware of the people around us; my mind would race. *Do they know he is gay? Do they think I condone his behavior? How does my associating with him affect me and my family?*

Stirring HIV into the mix greatly increased my anxiety. I had a family to worry about, but my two kids loved their Bubby. Gay and HIV were meaningless words to them. But for me it required suppressing all the hype surrounding Gays and HIV and deciphering truth from misinformation. I knew I could not suppress these concerns, feelings and moral conflicts indefinitely. So I was relieved God gave me time alone to talk to Him and listen to His response during the trip to Texas.

The sun was setting as we passed Moses Lake, Washington. The sky was turning a reddish pink and the grass was gold. The scenery seemed to go on forever and the bus tires on the asphalt made for an eerie pseudo-silence as I fell into my own world. For the next four hours I listened and God reminded me of what He had done for me. As we wound through the hills and valleys I felt His presence and saw the beauty of what He had created. As I drifted into my thoughts the bright evening colors slowly turned into dusk and then darkness. As the lights faded my mood and thoughts turned to the darker thoughts of what might happen. I had many questions, but no answers.

At day break we were in Billings, Montana. I had a long layover and I had time to relax and observe what was happening around me. People-watching is a normal characteristic for Sarah, she never misses anything, but I usually ignore the people around me and try not to be noticed by them. This morning was different. A family at the station was putting their son on the bus. They were much like my own family. The mother was very affectionate and huggy; the younger kids were just happy to be there to send their older brother off. The father was close-by but not interacting much with the family. When the son got on the bus everyone gave him a hug, but the son and father kept their emotions in check.

This interchange made me review the difference of my interaction between Jon, my foster son, and Jonathon, my five-year-old adopted son. The former was like the father and son at the bus station and the latter was like the mother and son. This started me thinking of my standards for accepting an adopted son and my Heavenly Father's standard to me as His adopted son. My acceptance of Jonathan was unconditional, like God's love for me. Yet my acceptance of Jon Michael required works and renunciation of his life-style. I had many questions, few answers and little time to resolve them.

As I boarded another bus and found a comfortable position, my mind drifted back to the previous September at SeaTac airport. We were putting Jon on a plane bound for Texas. At the gate Jon hugged his Mom tightly and she kissed him. He scooped Jonathan into his arms and I watched, detached, as little Jonathan put his chubby hands on his brother's face. Sierra stood beside him, her arms around his middle, her head snuggled into his side. The boarding call sounded and Jon got out his ticket. As he approached the gate, he turned and looked at me. We could not meet each other's eyes. Neither of us could reach out to hug the other. We stood there frozen for what seemed like an eternity. I spoke first, "Have a safe trip, son." "You, too," he responded in a quiet voice.

We waited at the gate, allowing the children to see their brother's plane fly off into the distance. As we left the terminal, I felt a twinge of guilt. Sarah noticed my discomfort and asked, "Honey, are you okay?"

I could only answer, "I wish I'd hugged him."

****

Late that evening I arrived in Arlington, Texas. Jon had attended an HIV/AIDS support group at a local church. Sarah had made arrangements through the pastor of the church for a person we had never met to pick me up at the bus station. I could never have done that on my own. When he offered to provide me with a place to stay, Sarah jumped at the hospitality. Out of pride, I would have declined and stayed at a hotel. But this kind stranger took me to his house for the night and to Jon's apartment the next day. How does Sarah so easily acknowledge and flow with what God has set in motion?

When I arrived at Jon's apartment, things were heating up between Jon and Ed. They were fighting over some trivial matter. Ed didn't acknowledge me, said some choice words to Jon, and stomped out angrily without saying anything to me. When Jon came down from the upstairs bedroom I was surprised to see how much weight he had lost since we had last seen him in

Sarah Pennington

September. His face was drawn and his movements were stiff. As he navigated the stairs his limbs displayed the jerky, animated gestures of an old man.

Jon had been sick, and arguing with Ed had left him in a bad mood. Ed had refused to help him pack, and Jon wasn't ready to leave for the trip home. In fact he wasn't sure that he *should* come home. I asked him if everything was okay between him and Ed, but he wasn't interested in talking about it. I dropped the matter and started to help him get his things together. Jon owned an Audi so he didn't have much room for his things and ended up leaving a lot of things he didn't want Ed to have. After the car was packed, true to form, Jon wouldn't leave until the apartment was clean and in order. Since he was mad at Ed, however, he pettily left the kitchen garbage can half-full.

The Journey Home

It was afternoon before we left Arlington. Since I had been traveling and Jon was still feeling poorly we stopped early for the night. Jon being Jon, he would only stay at Holiday Inn or Ramada Inn -- even though I had told him we were going to be tight on funds. Cleanliness was important to him and he liked to inspect the room before we settled in. Sarah always tells people that I have a receipt reviewed before we get from the grocery store check-out to the car. Well, Jon can have a room inspected and evaluated in one walk around the room. Not me -- I would forget about it and let it go. I just want a good night's sleep. Jon, however, would advise management about any discrepancy and ask the staff to correct it. We had some fruitless conversations about that during the trip.

The next morning we got an early start, which made me feel hopeful -- until we stopped for breakfast. We found a small restaurant near the freeway, which was crowded.

The host said it would be a while before a table opened, and promised to clear one as soon as possible. Jon said he was tired and needed to sit down. He looked around and saw an open seat in the waiting area. He walked over and asked if he could sit down. The people moved over to make additional room. As he was sitting down, he said, "I sure get tired more quickly since I caught the AIDS bug."

Everyone around him stopped and stared at him. One parent made the excuse, "We are running late and need to get going." Another patron said, "I'm not really hungry; I can get something later." In a matter of minutes, everyone was gone from the waiting area and nearby tables. The host came back calling a name, then stopped and looked around. He asked, "Where did everyone go? Jon looked around, shrugged his shoulders and said, "Hmmm. They were here a minute ago." He looked at me, smiled, and said to the host, "We're ready."

After breakfast we hit the road. It was a nice sunny day and it seemed to lift Jon's spirits. We talked briefly about the restaurant incident. I asked him why he had been so offensive. He said, "They were all looking at me and wondering, so I thought I would end the suspense. Besides, I was hungry and didn't want to wait."

"But" I asked, "didn't you care what they would think?"

"No. I didn't know anyone and I will never see them again. It probably will be my only fun today."

Sarah Pennington

The day flew by as we made good time. The conversation was on and off, and not strained. Normally when I feel uncomfortable I force the conversation and talk about nothing and avoid anything about me or my family. Today we talked a little about each other, but mostly about Weebok (the puppy he'd given Sierra and Jonathan) and Mom.

We stopped at Denny's several times during the trip, because they were open to finding a private and safe place where Jon could set up his IV. We have remained faithful to Denny's for their compassion during the trip. During those first years of the AIDS epidemic; hospitals, doctor's offices and medical clinics – the ideal places to perform an IV drip – were leery of the legal responsibility and would not host us.

When we stopped for the night, we stayed in a Holiday Inn, since Ramada Inn had had problems meeting Jon's expectation of getting soap scum out of the bathtub and they didn't fold the toilet paper into a point on the end the way Jon liked it. The Holiday Inn got a better grade, but they didn't fold the toilet paper to Jon's liking either.

The next morning we were slow getting up and getting ready to leave. We had a quick breakfast at Burger King (I didn't want a repeat of yesterday) and got on the road. I was still driving, and the highway seemed to go on forever. Jon was dozing on and off during the day, so I had a lot of time to reflect on how our lives were going to change over the next few months and years.

I was more concerned and worried about the years after he was gone. Jon was coming home because of Mom, and she knew it. Jon also knew that we would walk through this with him, even though we knew the emotional and social pain could be great. It was killing me to think I would deliberately impose that pain on Sierra and Jonathan. I didn't know how Sarah and I would handle this, so how could I ask a fifteen-year-old and a five-year-old to understand?

My mind kept going back to what drew Sarah to Jon and why the bond was so strong between them. Their backgrounds and lives were completely different yet many of their traits were similar. Jon could make her so mad she could spit, yet she still loved him to death. The bottom line was my relationship with Jon, good or bad, would affect everyone in my family and how I handled it was critical. My normal mode of sitting on the fence and letting things develop before making a decision was no longer an option. I had two days to resolve these concerns and make those decisions.

Jon woke up and it was time for a late lunch.

We stopped at a busy truck stop for lunch with a lot of people coming and going. Everyone seemed in a hurry to get wherever they were headed, so

Tap Dancing on Quicksand While Gargling Peanut Butter

some were impatient with the waiters and anxious to get their meals. After we were seated, Jon noticed a couple of truckers looking our way. He was sure they were talking about him. They would look our way, one of them would say something, and they would smile, shake their head, or chuckle. Jon surveyed the restaurant to see if any one else appeared to be paying attention to us. I wasn't much help. I tried to distract him, but I was flustered too, since I thought every one that looked at us assumed we were both gay and Jon had AIDS. Nonetheless, Jon kept an eye on the two truckers and commented, "It would be nice to have Brandy[9] here to put them in their place. I was glad he had left his Brandy getup in Texas and was praying that Jon wouldn't decide to make one of his snide comments to the big, burly truckers. Ten minutes later they paid for their meal and left. I sighed with relief and finished my meal.

We traveled non-stop until about ten that evening, and I wanted to stop for the night, but there were no hotels available which met Jon's criteria. We kept traveling. At eleven, I was completely given out and told Jon that we were going to stop at the next motel for the night. At the next exit there was a small family-run motel with individual cottages. It had a rustic décor, which did not endear it to Jon. The room was only thirty dollars which was an immediate red flag for Jon. Before we checked in he said that if we stayed there, he would probably die from catching some infectious disease. After all, he complained, he had AIDS and was susceptible to them. I was too tired to care and took the room anyway. It was a nice, cozy cabin and I thought it was adequately clean. Jon inspected the room and said there was no way he was going to sleep there. I told him he was more likely to get killed from me crashing the car or me strangling him than from any infectious disease he would catch. It was almost midnight by then, and I lay down on the bed and went to sleep.

At three, Jon woke me and said, "I have the car packed and it's time to leave." I told him I was too tired to drive, but he informed me he was going to drive. I dragged myself to the bathroom to wash my face. It was then I noticed a nice spring scent that wasn't there when we checked in. I looked around and the whole bathroom had been super-cleaned and the bedroom furniture had been wiped down and the windows cleaned. I looked in the trash can and it was full of sterile cleaning cloths that we had bought for the trip home. I asked Jon why we had to leave now if he had just cleaned and sterilized everything, but he still insisted we leave. I reluctantly got into the car and we left.

Jon was speeding along the country road that connected us to the freeway. Even though I was half asleep I noticed how the moonlight reflected off the fence along the road, and the small patches of fog. In the moon's glow you could see the landscape.

---

[9] Brandy was Jon's persona in drag – a beautiful cross-dressed version of himself – who won him first runner-up in the Miss Gay Alaska contest.

Sarah Pennington

As I looked over at Jon, the moonlight coming through the sunroof made him appear skinnier and extremely pale. This picture would come back to haunt me a few months later when he was on his death bed. Sarah couldn't understand why I avoided his room, but that was not the picture I wanted to remember of Jon. I would find other ways to comfort him in those last days.

Since I wasn't sure how capable Jon was to drive I stayed awake and we talked all night. We didn't talk about anything earth shattering, emotional or personal, but the talk was sincere and came easy.

Jon seemed anxious to get home, so we skipped breakfast and just picked up some snacks when we stopped to get gas. I kept dropping off to sleep and the morning passed quickly. Around noon I took over driving and Jon got some sleep. It was obvious the trip was taking its toll on him.

By four in the afternoon we were both hungry for a real meal. We stopped at a national chain-restaurant. I dropped Jon off at the door and went to park the car. As I approached the front door, Jon came out and said we needed to go somewhere else. I asked what happened and he wouldn't say, but it was obvious that they had refused him service. I told him we could go back and demand service, which startled me, because at the beginning of the trip I didn't even want to be seen with him in a public place for fear of reprisal and guilt by association. Now I was ready to advocate for him.

However, Jon was tired and depressed; he hadn't had his IV, and needed to leave. We found a Denny's a couple of exits down and Jon was able to take his IV, and get something to eat. Jon's spirits increased and he felt physically better. After we left Denny's, Jon said since we were less than seven hours from home he just wanted to drive straight through. We switched driving duties back and forth, and drove through the night. As we passed through Everett, Washington, barely an hour from home, I started to wish that we still had some time left alone. I knew once we got home Sarah and the kids would take over his life and he would bathe in their warmth and love.

As we took the Whidbey Island exit off I-5, I felt a peace and for the first time had a glimpse of the type of love that Jesus was talking about. Sarah and the kids had fully accepted Jon as part of the family. I, on the other hand, had welcomed Jon because of them, but hadn't accepted him. This trip had taught me to respect Jon for who he was, and we tried to make time for each other after we got home. Jon would facilitate this by buying me a truck-of-many colors – a fixer-upper of a farm truck that I was proud of, not because of how it ran or how it looked, but because my son, who loved me, purchased it for me. That old truck gave us something to do together and gave me many fond memories.

Tap Dancing on Quicksand While Gargling Peanut Butter

During the trip the Lord had taught me to take the beam out of my eye before I became concerned about the splinter in my son's eye.[10] I had always been surrounded by a large family that accepted me and loved me in spite of my short-comings. Jon, on the other hand, came from an abusive, dysfunctional family, which had abandoned and rejected him. I was amazed as I realized how much I loved Jon and accepted him as my son.

The trip home was profound for Jon and me. It enabled both of us to share his last months in a united and loving home. He came home to a father who loved him, and I came home to a house that felt like home.

---

[10] Matthew 7:3

April 2, 1994
Tacky, Tacky, Tacky

I didn't hear the sound of the car tires on the gravel driveway, or the footsteps as my guys entered the house. Papa had to find me upstairs in the big old farmhouse. Happy to have our family whole again, we embraced quickly and Papa said, "There's someone downstairs who wants to see you."

I couldn't descend the stairs fast enough. My son was home! I flew around the corner and almost collided with Jon. My heart stopped. The last time I'd seen him he'd weighed 165 pounds. The waif in front of me was less than 100 pounds. His first words were, "We need to go shopping – none of my clothes fit." To the bitter end, Jon was determined to be fashionable and meticulous. Tonight, however, he was anything but a fashion plate. He was shoeless and his jeans hung out over his feet like a Dr. Seuss character. Even though he'd belted them, the waist hung low on his hips – way before it was fashionable to show your boxers.

Jon had turned thirty-one on March 24, and here he stood wasted and gaunt, ready to crash and burn.[11] I helped Jon settle into his room, and he set up his IV drip for the night. I checked on Sierra and Jonathan, who were sleeping soundly, before Papa and I retired to our room. The full impact of what we had undertaken hit me full force, and I was scared to death.

When I came downstairs the next morning to make coffee, I expected Jon Michael to still be sleeping. Instead I heard, "Tacky, tacky, tacky," echoing in the master bathroom. The door was open and I stuck my head in. "Mother! Why haven't you replaced this hideous excuse for wallpaper?" Jon blatantly ripped a corner of wallpaper from the wall "Stop that! I don't have the time or money to replace it right now! Stop it!" "I'll replace it for you. This stuff is tacky, tacky, tacky!" While Jon enjoyed interior decorating and had excellent taste, the refinishing of my bathroom never happened. Actually, I liked the bright green and white seventies pattern. I didn't want to replace it. I didn't know that a short three months later that wallpaper would be a pertinent part of my grieving.

---

[11] Crashing and burning is a common term among AIDS patients. It refers to what feels like an overnight process – that moment when the airborne jet loses engine power and hits the tarmac.

Angels Around Me

As Jon's condition worsened, he could no longer mix the medication for his IV drip. I had to learn to manage his meds. In addition to the drip he was taking thirty-six pills each day.

I was grateful for the In-Home nurses who ministered to us those last two months teaching me and encouraging me. They were my rock and my comfort. While the nurses were dispatched from the south and central sections of the island, we lived at the north end, separating me from immediate access.

I had watched the nurse complete the Groshong procedure only once when Jon Michael's tube became clogged with a blood clot. The nurse was an hour away. On the phone, she told me what to do and talked me through drawing the clotted blood out of his tube and discarding the needle in the biohazard container. I filled another syringe with saline and flushed out the tube. When I withdrew the needle, I carelessly tried to put the cap back on the needle, which slipped and went into my middle finger to the bone. My son began to cry. I began to recite, "He has encamped His angels around me. I shall not be harmed... He has encamped His angels around me. I shall not be harmed..." Terrified, I thrust my hand under the kitchen faucet, allowing cool, soothing water to wash away the blood I frantically squeezed from my throbbing finger.

When I finally returned to the phone, the nurse was patiently waiting. Her voice was gentle and calming. Only then did I have the presence of mind to realize the needle I had stuck in my finger was the saline needle that I had used to flush out the Groshong tube and not the one that I had used to remove the blood clots. I did not make the same mistake again. Were there angels around me, protecting me? You betcha!

Sarah Pennington

May, 1994

The Last Hurrah

During April and May Jon spent as much time as possible making friends and socializing.

Our friend, Paula, had boarded her dog, Precious, with us. She came every day to feed, water and exercise the big, old huffalump of a huggy-dog. Paula and Jon became fast friends and would have long talks, and go out for coffee or dinner.

He explored our small downtown shopping area and found a quaint antique store. He struck up a conversation with the owner/manager and soon was decorating her windows and walls and stocking shelves for her.

Most importantly, Jon began to establish relationships among clergy. I was amazed one day when I asked him who he had been talking to on the phone. It was the pastor of a local church who met him in town and now was calling once a week to check on him. I would hear bits of their conversations on several occasions and revel at hearing Jon Michael talking about spiritual things.

A group of about twenty came to our house from Faith Temple Christian Center and had a prayer-walk around our property. We told Jon they were coming and he wanted no part of it. He didn't care if they prayed for him, "Just don't bug me with it, okay?"

The pastors and congregation of Faith began their walk around our acreage. A rainbow church of every race, their music was Black gospel. As they strolled and sang, some praying out loud, Jon was hooked. His favorite singer was Whitney Houston. He began to edge closer to the group.

Once inside the house, we gathered in the living room, held hands and prayed. There were large picture windows on two sides of the living room and the pastor's wife, my dear friend from MOPS, saw Jon pacing outside the windows, listening. She walked outside and sat on the back steps until Jon came to sit beside her. They talked for a while and she invited him in. I was shocked and blessed when he, on his own, walked to the center of the room and received a hug from one of the ministers and allowed the group to lay hands on him and pray. Jon had found a safe haven, separate from Mom and Dad, where he knew he was welcome.

Soon afterward, New Covenant Fellowship planned a church-wide picnic. When the phone rang the night before, I cringed as I heard, "I'm calling as a representative of the church."

Tap Dancing on Quicksand While Gargling Peanut Butter

I thought, Here it comes. I was relieved when I heard, "We just want to make sure that Jon Michael is coming tomorrow." The concern was not about his disease; rather I was asked what could be done to make Jon the most comfortable. In return I was able to comfortably offer those things I could do to ease any discomfort amidst the congregation. I would make Jon's plate for him and stay nearby during the picnic.

At the picnic we chose a table for our family. Jon was weak and spent most of his time at the table beside me. Throughout the afternoon a steady stream of folks came to sit with us, talk with Jon about his travels, his interests. I watched gratefully as he interacted with people who truly cared. Jon was having the opportunity to see that Christians, real Christians, were not like his birth-dad – the church deacon who had brutalized him. In spite of the religious media frenzy condemning those churches that were ministering to AIDS patients, he was able to see there were, indeed, compassionate Christians.

I, too, was able to reflect during the picnic. Though one church had turned their back on us – there would be five churches that touched our lives during our journey; as well as discreet members of our former church who called, sent cards and stood in the gap[12] for us.

I am especially grateful to two friends. Michele Mattson dropped by almost daily to check on me, do laundry and give me a shoulder to lean on. Paula Van Cott was tending to her dog, Precious, daily and would visit with Jon and give me a break. I love them both dearly.

Still, we learned one truly sad fact during our AIDS Journey – we knew many Christians who had met Jesus, but had not embraced His teachings of grace and forgiveness.

---

[12] In this incidence, to 'stand in the gap' refers to those who interceded in prayer for our safety.

Sarah Pennington

Crashing and Burning

As the growth and viral infection in Jon's lung began to permeate his bronchial system, and travel up his glands to his brain, his behavior became more and more erratic. Morbid humor, the advice of other 'AIDS moms', our support group, and the prayers of fellow Christians got me through.

As Papa and I realized how quickly my time would be totally consumed by Jon's care, we made special time for Sierra and Jonathan – and for ourselves. Jon's emotional state was regressing to child-like jealousy and possessiveness. Worse, he began to tantrum. I'll share one, of several incidents.

One night Papa took me to the theatre to see the Tom Hanks movie, "Philadelphia." It was therapeutic for both of us. As Denzel Washington's character watched Tom Hanks sing an aria, I glanced over to see a tear glistening down Papa's face. We are from the last generation of "Men don't cry." It would be the only time I would actually see him grieve during our journey.

When we arrived home that evening, we discovered one of Jon's most memorable tantrums. He had been left alone. He did not like it. He had taken his pill box, a large monstrosity containing thirty-six pills for thirty days – a total of 1,080 capsules and tablets and dumped them into my big, green Tupperware bowl. The health nurse and I had filled it the day before. It would be days before she'd be back. There was nothing I could do until morning. Jon would have to make it through the night with only his IV drip.

I cried out in frustration, "Jon, what have you done?"

"It's amazing," he said, "that no one around me is as intelligent as I am. Did you forget that I'm dying? I have AIDS, remember? I need my mother to be here – not off socializing." He picked up a handful of pills saying, "I'm dying anyway, I'll just take them all."

There was no motherly gentleness in my voice as I ordered Jon to get his bunnies to his room so I could set up his IV. I told Jon, "We'll talk about this in the morning after I've calmed down."

"Aren't you going to tell me you're sorry for leaving me all alone?"

"NO!"

The next morning, Jon admitted, "That was really irrational, wasn't it." I agreed and used the opportunity to take his car keys, explaining that I would be spending most of my time with him for a while and would be the one driving. He never forgave me for taking away his car – his last link to normalcy.

Tap Dancing on Quicksand While Gargling Peanut Butter

I called our pharmacist, who graciously agreed to meet me on his lunch break. He was prepared with a printed copy of Jon's meds and the dosages. As he identified and sorted the pills and capsules, he informed me of the dosages and I filled the compartments of the monthly planner box.

It was during this time period that an incident happened which was prophetic. One day as I received ten of Jon Michael's prescriptions from the pharmacy clerk, I overheard a lady behind me whisper, "Wow, that's a lot of medication!"

Five-year-old Jonathan was with me. He turned to the lady and in his exuberant, cherubic voice said, "My bubby Jon has AIDS. He's gonna die, but it is okay, 'cause he's gonna live with Jesus!" The lady stooped to Jonathan's level and said, "Out of the mouths of babes!"[13] Spontaneously, she hugged him as he smiled.

Those joyful moments were a much needed balance for the days of transition, when Jon was losing muscle control and refusing to wear Depends. On the worst day, I cleaned diarrhea off the six surfaces of his bathroom eighteen times.

Mean as it may sound, the next morning I handed him a pack of Depends and said, "Wear them, or clean the bathroom!"

"But, Mom, my skin is so thin and sensitive. You wouldn't make me clean with Clorox."

"Try me!"

Depends became part of his daily routine.

---

[13] Psalm 8:2

Don't Come Home

It was during those days of chaos that I called my mother (Miss Gladys) for support. She had no idea what we were experiencing. Papa had chosen to keep our trial from his family until after Jon's death. I chose to call Mother on a regular basis, but to withhold the gory details.

Maybe, if I'd been more forthright with her, she would have postponed our conversation. Nonetheless, she advised me, "Your brother doesn't think ya'll should come back down here."

"Why?"

"He's afraid you'll give us AIDS."

I took a deep, cleansing breath and queried, "How do you feel, Mama?"

"Well," she said, "It's kind of embarrassing, you know. I hope you're not blabbing any of this to your aunts and uncles."

"No, don't worry, Mother, I won't embarrass you."

I was too exhausted and deflated to argue.

I didn't call again until Jon's death. A year and a half later we were allowed to visit but were asked to stay in a motel.[14]

---

[14] "When my father and my mother forsake me, then the Lord will take me up. Psalm 27:10

Tap Dancing on Quicksand While Gargling Peanut Butter

Hallucinations

Before Jon came home, Joe Accord, a counselor who gave his time to a support group for family and friends of those living with AIDS, suggested we see the movie "And the Band Played On." It chronicled the start of the HIV virus and its progression to an epidemic.

There is a poignant scene in the film where a gentleman who is babbling nonsensically, comes to his senses for a moment and says, "I'm talking gibberish, aren't I?" He immediately began talking gibberish again. When we talked about this phenomenon in our support group, one of the moms warned, "It will be the same with their hallucinations. They'll snap out of the delusions, acknowledge them, and go right back into them."

I asked her, "How do you deal with the hallucinations?"

She told me to just "Go with them. Become part of them. It will comfort your son." It was a welcomed wisdom.

I'm only going to share two hallucination experiences. There were several.

****

I got ready to go to bed, making sure the baby monitor was set so I could hear Jon if he needed me. Around two, my sleep was interrupted, not by the monitor, but by Jon's loud, "M-ooooo-th-eeeeee-r! Hurry up! We're gonna be late!"

I hurried down the stairs without grabbing my robe, wearing only my black, slip-style negligee, hoping to silence Jon before he woke up the whole family.

"Mom, I had a hard time getting them to open the Bon at this hour, so come on!" He began talking to a non-existent saleslady telling her the styles he'd like his mom to try on. In Jon's mind we were in the Bon Marche, with an entourage of ladies to assist his mom. He had taken me shopping on several occasions over the years and this would be our last big spree.

As he repeatedly extended his empty hand to me, I accepted the imaginary formal gown, dress, shoes, or hat he proffered and stepped into the dressing room (actually the dining room) to try them on. I would come back into the room in nothing but my black negligee and model for him.

As I modeled the gown he believed he was purchasing for me to wear on mine and Papa's anniversary, Jon stopped for a moment and asked, "I'm hallucinating, aren't I? Are you having fun, Mom? What are you doing shopping in your negligee?" I didn't have time to answer before he turned to the imaginary salesclerk and said, "We'll take this one. It's beautiful on her."

Sarah Pennington

On another evening, I heard Jon screaming and ran to the living room to find him flailing his arms and ducking.

"What's the matter, son?"

"The neighbor's horses are out and got in the house!"

I realized he was hallucinating again. One by one, I caught each horse and walked it to the back door where I told Jon the neighbor was waiting to take them home. When the last horse was gone, Jon fell into my arms sobbing, "It wasn't real Mom."

"No, son, it wasn't. You're okay. Let's go back to bed."

"Will you stay with me 'til I go to sleep?"

"Of course."

As I write today, I can feel the tug of his hand holding the front of my shirt, a gesture that he repeated many times that last month.

Late June, 1994
I Want to Be a Guinea Pig

Jon both surprised me and made me proud when he offered himself to the University of Washington (UW) for AIDS research.

As Jon's body was withering away and his headaches were intensifying, he allowed himself to be prodded, probed and tested. This was the early nineties and we knew *nothing* about AIDS.

The hospital was generous, providing us with an isolated room with an extra cot for me. Because we were still ignorant about the HIV virus, all the vents were sealed to our room, we were not allowed to have air conditioning, and the windows were locked. It hit 110 degrees in the room where I was required to wear a mask at all times.

I chose to make a quick three-hour round-trip drive to get some cooler clothes from home. When I returned to the hospital, a nurse met me as I got off the elevator and informed me with a grin that I was not allowed to leave again. "Anything you need," she added, "someone will fetch for you." I was puzzled until I found Jon sitting on the floor outside his room, his hospital garb all twisted, his Groshong compromised. He wouldn't let anyone near him and the staff had waited for my return for fear of hurting him or infecting themselves.

I held Jon, who clung to me crying, while a nurse cut him out of his getup and checked his Groshong. We re-dressed him and put him back to bed. Once he was settled he urged, "Mom, please promise you won't leave me again." I wish he could have promised me the same.

Sarah Pennington

July 1, 1994

Isn't it amazing how the human psyche can feel such intense pain and exquisite joy in the same breath without decomposing? Yet that phrase perfectly defines my feelings on July 1, 1994.

My precious 31-year-old son -- there he sat, on a bed at University of Washington Hospital looking like Mahatma Gandhi, his legs folded in a yoga-like position, his body skeletal. Our nurse had told us a wheelchair would arrive soon to transport Jon Michael downstairs for more tests. Painful tests. Tests for which he'd volunteered to be a guinea pig.

I hadn't wanted him to do this. I felt he had gone through enough pain as it was. "No, Mom," he'd said, "let's do this. We can't save me. I'm dying. But we can save another son's life and another mother's pain." Reluctantly, I had agreed. His one condition had been that I would stay round-the-clock with him. Papa stayed at home holding down the fort with a five-year-old son and a fifteen-year-old daughter.

This morning Jon seemed to have important things on his mind. "Mom," he said, "Can you pray with me?"

"Sure!" I wasn't sure what he wanted me to pray for, but I prayed an eloquent Southern-Baptist-thee-and-thou-prayer full of adjectives and extemporaneous muttle....Amen!"

With his familiar smirk, Jon responded, "That's nice, Mother; now tell me what I need to pray."

My heart came to my throat. Here we were at the moment I'd prayerfully requested for sixteen years — the experience that will be emblazoned on my memory until eternity -- the brief seconds when Jon Michael prayed after me, "Dear God, I have sinned and I am sorry for my sins. I acknowledge that Jesus is your precious son, who died for my sins. Please come into my life and sit on the throne of my heart. Amen."

As our tear-filled eyes locked on each other, an attendant entered the room and settled Jon Michael into a wheelchair. I offered a gentle wave and smiled as he was wheeled away. Sitting there on his hospital bed, clutching his security blanket, I wept tears of relief, joy and pain.

Exquisite joy. My precious son would soon enter eternity to redesign the robes of the angels to include mauve and aqua. The streets of gold will now have little silver speckles for pizzazz, and my room in that great mansion will now be decorated beyond my wildest imagination.

Intense pain. Within three weeks my son would be gone, the latest fatality in the AIDS epidemic.

Tap Dancing on Quicksand While Gargling Peanut Butter

July 2, 1994
Sierra's Sixteenth Birthday

On the afternoon of July first, Jon made a request to his primary physician, Dr. Raghu. "May I please check out for the weekend so I can attend my little sister's sixteenth birthday party?" Dr. Raghu complied, but warned me in the hallway that the trip could be too hard on Jon, and asked me to call his office on the fifth to let him know if we'd be returning. He thanked me for Jon's sacrifice and assured me there had been great value in the testing.

Jon was exhausted and needed both Sierra and me to walk him to the door and get him to bed. He and Sierra sat in his room that night and talked.

He told his little sister he was giving her his Audi for her birthday, but admonished her, "You can't have it until I can't drive it anymore."

I left them talking and went to bed.

When I woke on Saturday morning, July 2, I went downstairs to make coffee. I found Jon sitting criss-cross-applesauce on the living room sofa, emaciated and gaunt. I kissed his forehead and went back to the kitchen to start breakfast.

I heard a sickening noise, ran to the living room and found Jon on the floor on all fours in the throws of a grand mal seizure. I screamed for Papa who picked Jon up like a baby and sat with him on his lap until paramedics arrived.

The seizure subsided and Papa gently eased Jon onto the sofa. The paramedics took over, and kindly examined Jon, who was stiff and disoriented. The medic asked the necessary questions, 'What is your name? What day is it? How old are you? Who is the President of the United States?' Jon was unresponsive.

Sierra began to giggle. At first I thought she was just nervous. Then I saw her pointing at Jon's fisted hand. Totally perplexed at his inability to respond, or move, Jon had managed to extricate the middle finger of his right hand to express his frustration.

It was Sierra's sixteenth birthday. We spent it in the emergency room with Jon Michael. About mid-day it hit her. This was Jon's first seizure. He would no longer be able to drive. The Audi was hers. This was not the way she wanted to receive it.

July 4, 1994
Mama Sings the Star Spangled Banner

Months before Jon came home, I had been invited to sing the national anthem at our city's 10K Freedom Run. Understandably, I had totally spaced the commitment until I received a call from the coordinator to go over last minute details.

With Jon still disoriented and bed-ridden, I chose to fulfill my promise to sing. He never knew I was gone.

On the fifth, Jon said he wanted to return to UW. I called Dr. Raghu, who talked to Jon and obliged his request.

On the sixth, Jon sat up in his hospital bed and announced, "Mom! You have to go! You're supposed to sing today!" I gently explained that it was July 6, that I had not missed the singing engagement, and all was well.

Jon was frustrated that he'd lost three days and ordered me to sing for him. So, there I stood in an isolation room in the terminal ward of University of Washington Medical Center in cut-off jeans and a t-shirt and, just as I had done at the 10K, recited the story of Francis Scott Key before wailing out my red-neck rendition of "Oh say can you see, by the dawn's early light!"

The next seven days went quickly. Dr. Raghu was extraordinary. He sensed Jon's urgency to leave as much educational information as he could and wanted to honor that, while being sensitive to Jon's comfort.

Tap Dancing on Quicksand While Gargling Peanut Butter

July 13, 1994

Finally, I knew we'd had enough. I spoke with Dr. Raghu, and asked the pertinent questions, "What will more tests tell us?" "How will you use the information?" With no response worthy of Jon's pain, Dr. Raghu sent us home.

That last day at the hospital as we waited for discharge papers, Jon asked me for a favor. "Mom," he said, "from now 'til the day you die, promise me that every time you see a gay person you will tell them how much God loves them." I have done my best to keep that promise.

We had gone to the hospital on Wednesday. Jon had held my arm and walked to the car. The following Wednesday, Jon came home by ambulance, while I drove myself. On the way home I prayed, "God, I know this is selfish, but I need a sign from You that Jon didn't just do this for his mom. I need to know his salvation is real."

Sadly for Sierra, I had miscalculated, fully expecting to arrive home before the ambulance. In Sierra's sixteen-year-old naiveté, she had anticipated her Bubby getting better in the hospital, not worse. When the paramedics pulled him out of the ambulance on a stretcher, she was devastated. Her first words to me were, "Why didn't you warn me?"

July 16, 1994
Jon's Angels Appear

When our Dalmatian, Weebok, whined at the window to be let in, Jon asked me to raise his bed and open the door for her.

Weebok trotted into Jon's room and started toward him. Near the foot of the bed, she stopped abruptly, her ears shot up, her feet dug into the carpet like a balking donkey and she began to shake. I asked, "Weebok, what's the matter?" Jon responded, "Oh, she sees the angels," and motioned to either side of his headboard. I was disappointed that I could not see them (nor would I) and said so. Jon grinned and said, "Of course not, they're my angels."

Weebok backed slowly out of the room and sped down the hallway to where Sierra was lying on the living room love seat. Weebok took a flying leap, pounced on her, and whining, buried her face in Sierra's neck.

Weebok made several aborted attempts to re-enter Jon's room before she could go all the way to the side of the bed and let him pet her. Then she took up residence underneath the bed where she could ignore the existence of the Heavenly visitors.

During Jon's last five days with us, he continually acknowledged their presence and spoke with them. I never saw them. I only felt them consistently until he was gone.

I wanted so much to be able to talk to them, to ask questions only they could answer. During those sixteen years that I prayed "whatever it takes" for Jon's salvation, were these the angels who had intervened consistently in his life at my request? Were they sent to comfort and calm the fears of a 31-year-old man-child about to face his scariest challenge? While I live, I'll never know. "Now we see but a poor reflection as in a mirror; then we shall see face to face. Now I know in part; then I shall know fully, even as I am fully known."[15]

Until then, I am content to be grateful...

---

[15] 1 Corinthians 13:12 New International Version

Tap Dancing on Quicksand While Gargling Peanut Butter

Answered Prayer

His last seven days I was blessed to have Home Health nurses come in for eight hours each day. I chose 11pm-7am so I could sleep.

His body was skeletal. His pain was unspeakable. His emotional torment was unbearable to watch. Yet his dignity was intact. The rest of us were carried on angels' wings.

Jon progressively lost the use of his limbs and his bodily functions as the virus literally ate away his brain cells.

On Saturday evening, the visiting nurse told me Jon was her first AIDS patient and admitted she was a little nervous. I told her not to worry, showed her the baby monitor and instructed her to have Jon call my name if she had to deal with any body fluids or change a diaper, and I'd handle it. At two on Sunday morning I was awakened by his voice on the monitor praying the sinner's prayer with his nurse. As tears streamed down my face, I thanked God for the best confirmation He could have given me of Jon's salvation.

By noon on Sunday, Jon lost his ability to speak as the virus rapidly tore through his brain cells. The one ability that would not go away was the depth with which he looked into my eyes and the grip he used to hold and tug on my shirt.

Sarah Pennington

Last Days

Jon had purchased his dad the truck-of-many-colors. This was the young man who'd said, "I'd rather have a car in the driveway that looks nice and doesn't run, than drive something that looks like this." Now, he had purchased an old, well-kept, but many-colored farm truck. One which ran well, but looked awful.

During Jon's last days, as he lay bed-ridden and sliding in and out of consciousness, Papa parked the truck outside Jon's window where he could see his dad continuing the job they'd started together. It was the best gesture of love Papa could have given him. Jon had me move the position of his hospital bed so he'd have a better view of his dad sanding out the rough spots and priming the paint.

An exceptional father, Papa had placed Jonathan's Nintendo in a corner of Jon's room, allowing the five-year-old to play without the volume. Each time Jon awoke he'd look around the room for little Jonathan, who would take a short break to share hugs and cuddle.

Papa and I were concerned for Sierra. We knew our sixteen-year-old was having the hardest time. She would sit for long periods and hold Jon's hand. It was unbearable to see her face.

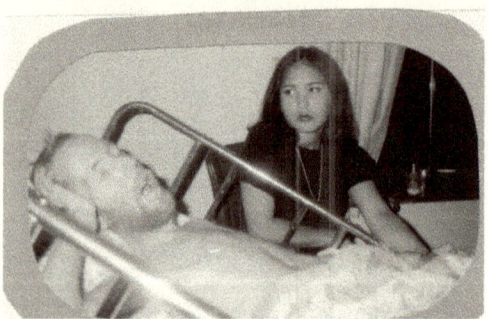

Jon and Sierra, July 20, 1994

Jon breathed his last earthly breath at 7:35 am on July 22, 1994. He was lying on my bosom, clinging to my shirt. I am eternally grateful to the two angels who took charge of him and led him into the presence of his Creator.

Tap Dancing on Quicksand While Gargling Peanut Butter

2008

At thirty, Sierra has a ten-year-old, Sean, whose name is a derivative of Jon and her six-year-old calls his big brother Bubby. She and I think of Jon when we smell a mauve Home Interiors candle, because he wanted them lit in the sconces on his wall those last days. We have been known to become tearful in the Safeway cookie aisle when we see Mother's Taffy cookies – Jon's favorite.

Over the years when Papa has been discouraged and worried about Sierra, he has wondered if he made the right choice when he brought Jon home. She had the most difficult time with Jon's death and went off the deep end the year Jon died. We are proud she has sobriety now, and continue to support her as she battles drugs and alcohol. Fourteen years after Jon's death, Papa knows it was a good decision.

Jonathan, who has only a few quality memories of his brother, honors him by being a son who treasures his dad and makes his mama proud. Papa is grateful for the time he had with Jon Michael and how God changed him during the trip to Texas. As a result, he raised Jonathan, by example, to be a man who openly shows affection to his family.

And me, the out-going, vocal, St. Bernard of our family? I continue to speak, sing and resonate the joy of Jon Michael's time with us.

He has left an indelible hand-print on our lives.

Sarah Pennington

Fifty Ways to De-Stress in Five Minutes or Less

I am very proud of my DHK (Doctor of Hard Knocks). I have been a foster parent, adoptive parent and a grandparent raising a grandchild non-stop for over thirty years. I have learned these techniques the hard way.

No matter what your philosophy or technique, breathing is the key. We breathe in peace and breathe out stress. We all need prayer and meditation, time to relax and reflect.

However, for those of us who are the parents or educators of children, we need split-second relief. These are fun to do with the kiddos, too.

1. Mount St. Helens: Become a volcano! Bend over and touch your toes. Begin to growl, increasing as you touch your knees, waist, and shoulders. Fling your arms skyward and release your roaring stress!

2. Bubbles: What a cheap way to blow out stress and brighten your spirits.

3. Blow Outs: As adults we need to remember to have fun. Party blow outs force us to exhale with hilarity. A lady in one of my presentations said she couldn't wait for the ride home so she could stop at a traffic light, look at the car next to her and show off her blow out.

4. Dance: Pop in a three to five minute CD and work that stress right out of your system!

5. The James Brown: Wooooooow! I feel good. Dooten dooten dooten doo… Clams the kids up in the car faster than you can scream it!

6. I am not crazy. Look in the mirror, make a ridiculous face and say, "I am not crazy, I will live through this, and I will still be sane!"

7. I love you. One of the hardest things we will ever do is look ourselves in the eye in the mirror. Do so anyway and say, "I love you." Repeat twice a day until you mean it.

8. Balloons: Blow them up. Sit on them. Pop them. Play with them.

9. Bouncy Ball: State your stress as you bounce the ball on the floor, e.g. "I cannot live through one more temper tantrum!"

10. Call a friend: Those simple words, "I'm having a rough day," when said to a friend, releases weight from our shoulders.

11. Recite from your faith:

Tap Dancing on Quicksand While Gargling Peanut Butter

- Christian: He has encamped His angels around me. I will not be harmed! Psalm 34:7
- Wiccan: Everything is as it should be.
- Alcoholics Anonymous: Until I accept that people, places and things are as they should be, I will not have peace.
- Buddhist: Come down Buddha, help me forgive!
- Teen Goth: If the world didn't suck, we'd all fall off!

12. Chocolate: One Hershey's kiss is only 25 calories. Sugar free chocolate is easy to find. Place one kiss on your tongue and savor it. Close your eyes. Breathe. Allow the fragrance of the chocolate, the taste of the chocolate, the essence of your breathing soothe your stress away.

13. Journal: This is one of the best survival techniques. Five minutes of writing what is on your mind releases the stress of it and gives you a memory tool for later.

14. Scrapbook: Yes, you can do a five-minute scrap booking project. Choose a set of six pictures or the paper and stickers to go with them.

15. Sex – Enough said.

16. Cup of Tea: Even while the kids continue to wail, a cup of tea soothes the harried soul. Sharing a cup of tea with one's teenager is a great diffuser.

17. Sing Silly Songs: We all know some. No? How about, "Nobody loves me, everybody hates me, I'm gonna go eat worms."

18. Shut Your Mouth and Breathe: When we get stressed we tend to open our mouths and shallow breathe. Focus on taking deep breaths with your mouth closed.

19. Five-Minute Workout: Put on music. Invite the kids to join you and just move!

20. Lotion: The act of applying lotion to our hands, feet, or face is a self-loving gesture. We feel special and smell better.

21. Massage: Share a shoulder rub with your spouse, child, or co-worker – or take time to rub your own neck, do neck and shoulder rolls.

22. Take a Hot or Cold Shower: Whatever your preference, a five-minute shower is a great rejuvenator and stress reducer.

23. Affirmations: "I can do this." "I am a beautiful woman inside and out." "I am loved." Write them on sticky notes and post them.

24. Throne of Humor: Keep humorous literature near the toilet.

25. Cry: When we are walking trials, it is healthy to release tears.

26. Give Your Stressor Five Minutes of Attention: Yep, just stop what you're doing and give that precious child your complete attention for five minutes. It's amazing how much they enjoy us and how much better we feel.

27. Play an instrument: No musical talent? Take up the kazoo! All you have to do is hum. Kazoos don't care if you're sharp, flat or out of tune.

28. Play with Legos, Lincoln Logs, or Barbies: Take five minutes to play with a child. Enjoy your inner child, while giving them a place to focus.

29. Write a Thank You note. Telling someone else what they mean to us lifts our spirits and reminds us of our blessings.

30. Hug someone. Especially the one giving you stress. Okay, not so hard. Whoa! You don't want to break a rib…

31. Paint/Color: I just finished a tempura paint kindergarten quality picture with sparkle accents, while the grandson made a nebula.

32. Plant something: Herbs in the kitchen window, seeds for the summer, just do it!

33. Take out the Garbage: Yeah, really. Taking out the trash means you have to go outside and walk. If you are *really* stressed, you can *really* slam that garbage into the trash can.

34. Jump Rope: Not me, but you go for it!

35. Take a five-minute walk: The art of walking away from a stressful situation is priceless.

36. Play a computer game: Be careful. Five minutes means a hand of solitaire, or minesweeper. Another gimmick is having a free download that's expired and let's you play for five minute sessions.

37. Put your face in a pillow and scream: Enough said.

38. Make funny faces: Do this with a partner or in the mirror. Laugh out loud.

39. Take pictures: It's amazing how much more pleasant people become when we start taking pictures.

40. Make a grateful list: On your worst day, pull out a notebook and begin writing down the good stuff. The bad things will start to look smaller and short-term.

41. Streamers: Those wonderful little plastic or wooden sticks with long metallic streamers on them are so much fun. Put on your favorite praise, country, or rock music and make some joy.

Tap Dancing on Quicksand While Gargling Peanut Butter

42. Listen to quiet music. Nature tapes or easy listening is soothing during chaotic days.

43. Dust: Remember the guy in the Karate Kid sing-songing, "Wipe on, wipe off?" Instead, make an exercise of your dusting, "Breathe in, stress gone."

44. Go to your happy place: Close your eyes. Where are you? At the beach? Gone fishing? At the spa getting a cucumber facial peel? Riding a horse into the wind?

45. Have a glass of red wine or grape juice: Both work to relax you and are good for your heart.

46. Plan a date: When life is bombarding us, it is wise to have something to look forward to. A date includes another person, laughter and good conversation. A date can be with your spouse, significant other, girl or guy friend, or one of your children. It only takes five minutes to make a phone call, check the entertainment section of the paper, or make a reservation.

47. Laugh out loud: It is a common, if unproven knowledge. Laughing out loud not only relieves stress and lifts our spirits, but is good for the heart, and a cancer preventative.

48. Talk to the wall: Sometimes things build up that don't need to be said to anyone. Go to a place where no one can hear you and let it out. The best part is that the wall won't talk back, argue, tell you to get off your pity pot, or negate your feelings. Walls can be very good friends. They are totally unmoved by your ranting and raving and they'll be right there welcoming you the next time you need to yell.

49. Post love notes: Many times the ones we love most are the ones who stress us most. Posting little love notes reminds us and them why we love them.

50. Do a good deed. Write a note of encouragement. Do one of the kid's chores. Pop something in the oven for a shut-in or neighbor. You'll feel better, I promise.

And my bonus – the phrase my children hate to hear – "This too, shall pass."

Angel Hugs,
Sarah

Sarah Pennington

www.ingramcontent.com/pod-product-compliance
Lightning Source LLC
Chambersburg PA
CBHW021025090426
42738CB00007B/909